NONNA'S

strada della

NONNA

PASSION, PARMESAN AND A SIX FOOT ROLLING PIN

Dedications

This book is dedicated to my mother Tiziana and, of course, my Nonna Andreina De Col-Grazi whose passion and hard work inspired me to open Nonna's and now to produce this book. Both are no longer with us, but I'm sure are looking down on our every move.

To my Italian aunties - Gabby and Lidia.

For my wife, Melanie, who without a quibble has put up with me not only on the adventure of this book, but has stood by me throughout the many hours and years on the rollercoaster of establishing Nonna's.

The rest of my family's support; my stepson Ross, my brother Rene and my sister Siobhan, my in-laws, Janet and Les. To a true gentleman my father, Gerry, who loved nothing better than sitting at the end of the bar with a glass of vino and plate of prosciutto, watching his son's business thrive. He was always there when needed.

Of course Maurizio who shared the belief at the onset and still believes in the vision.

The team at Nonna's; the chefs Jamie Taylor, Paul Crossland and the rest of the boys for helping out on the recipes and food shots in this book. To all past chefs, especially Nic Long.

To Daniel Jackson, general manager, for sharing the belief, and to the rest of the crew too many to mention that make Nonna's what it is.

A special thank you to Chiara Albrizio for her invaluable help with putting this book together and always being a multitasker when needed.

Jodi Hinds for her fabulous photography and to the team at the Regional Magazine Company – Andy Waple, Martin Edwards and Paul Cocker – for their creative input that made this book possible.

To Martino Maniero from Deli Italia, our main supplier and now a firm friend, and to Moreno Mori for all his help over the years, especially with building Casa di Nonna's.

Paolo Brady for help and advice on various matters over the years.

A final big thank you to all our loyal customers who have supported us in everything we have tried to do at Nonna's; without them we would be nothing.

Gian Bohan

"Nonna" Andreina De Col-Grazi

1918 - 2004

Contents

When we opened Nonna's in 1996 we had the ambition to share our passion of authentic Italian foods and the country's fabulous and diverse wines with the British public.

We had no great business plan, just a desire to bring the true taste of Italian life and its culture to our part of the world.

There were plenty of Italian restaurants in Sheffield and there was a strong, tight-knit community of Italians who had come to Britain mainly to work in restaurants.

But there was no true, authentic taste of those things we took for granted – the real flavour of the country that our parents, and generations of our families before them, had nurtured.

It was our dream to open the eyes of the British public to creamy cappuccinos, strong dark espressos and the delights of traditional mortadella, parmesan and pastas of all shapes and sizes.

We had no idea where our dream would lead us when we bought the former butcher's shop on the corner of Ecclesall Road and Hickmott Road.

With the traditional culinary skills of our Italian ancestors to fall back on and with the support of our parents, families and friends, Nonna's was born.

This is a story not only of how our dream came true, but also of the food, wines and culture of the country that inspires us.

Gian Bohan & Maurizio Mori

CHAPTER one

Nonna has arrived.... BUONGIORNO!

The story of Nonna's could never have been told had it not been for the inspiration of my granny.

Andreina De Col-Grazi, known to me as "Nonna", was a typical Italian lady of her generation – an expert in the kitchen.

She could wield her huge rolling pin with ease, producing big sheets of pasta in a flash.

As a young boy growing up with my Italian mother and Irish father in their adopted city of Sheffield, I used to watch her with awe at work producing sheets of lasagne.

Nonna lived all her life in Modena, the historic town in Emilia-Romagna, where she had a little deli.

Every year, especially at Christmas, she would visit us in Sheffield with my grandfather.

Their arrival was always a spectacular affair.

Grandfather would pull his Alfa Romeo onto the drive, fling open the car boot to reveal a cornucopia of treasures. The aromas of mortadellas, salamis, prosciutto di Parma, chunks of parmesan and other delicacies would waft from the car.

"Smell these melons," grandfather would insist, pushing a pair of the strange looking lightly-ribbed pale green fruits under our noses; "You can't get fresh melons like these over here!"

Italy had come to Sheffield and my sister Siobhan, brother Rene and myself were in heaven.

Early in the morning we would get out of bed and watch Nonna at work in the kitchen.

With her legendary rolling pin she would get to work making pasta. We still have it hanging from the wall in our Cucina. When I was a small child that rolling pin seemed to be well over six feet long!

She would use dozens of eggs to make three kilos of pasta which she would roll out, seemingly with ease across our kitchen table.

There is a very distinct art to making pasta with a rolling pin. By the time she had finished, there was a sheet of creamy-coloured pasta four feet across stretched out like a table cloth.

She would fold it like a curtain and slice it at an angle for tagliatelle or cut into small squares for tortellini or larger sheets for lasagne. The off-cuts and scraps were made into maltagliati for use in pasta e fagioli, a soup made with borlotti beans and vegetables.

Granny was like a machine, she was so good at making pasta, especially lasagne, for which she was a legend.

These days hand rolled pasta making is sadly a dying art because it is so difficult to perfect and it's time consuming.

This was the start of my love affair with Italy that was bonded by family connections and many happy childhood memories.

Our family would visit Nonna and grandfather in Modena where we learned much about Italian foods, wines and its culture.

We were young, impressionable, inquisitive children and were exposed to the sights and smells of some extraordinary local produce.

Being surrounded by unfamiliar things, such as enormous mortadellas, salamis, whole wheels of parmesan cheese, left me with lasting memories.

And then there was Nutella…

The sweet, gorgeous creamy chocolate and hazelnut spread had never reached our shores when I first saw it in Modena.

As a young child I would dip my fingers into these big jars of Nutella, before enjoying mortadella sandwiches washed down with succo di frutta, the nectar-thick juice.

It was in Modena that I learned from a very early age that quality ingredients were the key to the gates of paradise.

"Nonna was a typical Italian lady of her generation – an expert in the kitchen."

prosciutto DI PARMA
& CULATELLO DI ZIBELLO

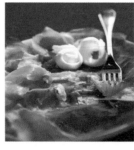

Prosciutto di Parma is a product known worldwide. Our friend Alberto Medici, of the wine and balsamic vinegar makers Medici Ermete, chaperoned us on a tour of the Conti's Parma ham factory in Langhirano, a town in the province of Parma in Emilia-Romagna.

Here we learned the full story of how the local pigs are reared before being slaughtered, cured and turned into one of the greatest of delicacies.

The story begins with a careful selection of the animals. Parma pigs must be either the Large White, Landrace or Duroc breeds, born and raised in just 11 regions of central-northern Italy.

Their diet is a specially regulated blend of grains and cereals, even the whey from Parmigiano-Reggiano cheese production, ensuring a heavy pig with a moderate daily growth in an excellent state of health.

They must be at least nine months old and a minimum of 140 kgs at the time of slaughter.

Parma ham is an all-natural product; additives such as sugar, spices, smoke, water and nitrites are strictly prohibited.

It takes a long time to turn the meat into succulent ham. Only the rear haunches are used and the curing is controlled carefully so that the ham absorbs only enough salt to preserve it. By the end, a trimmed ham will have lost more than a quarter of its weight through moisture loss, helping to concentrate the flavour. Over time the meat becomes tender and the distinctive aroma and flavour emerge.

While Prosciutto di Parma is widely known and appreciated, fewer people outside Italy know of Culatello di Zibello, a very special ham which we tasted at Trattoria La Buca.

Like Parma ham, Culatello di Zibello, is a DOP product, a symbol meaning its authenticity is protected by European Union regulations and its production is guarded and controlled by the "Consorzio per la Tutela del Culatello di Zibello."

Only the very heart of the haunch of a Parma ham is used – it is the muscle of the animal that is least used, so it's much more tender. After de-boning and trimming the extra fat, the ham is tied for the first time, sprinkled with salt and massaged patiently so that the salt begins to be absorbed.

It is then left to cure in cellars. At a later stage, the ham is put in pig bladders, skilfully sewn onto the meat. The Culatello gains its unmistakable fragrance and flavour thanks to the micro-climate along the banks of the River Po in the province of Parma noted by cold, damp and foggy winters and hot, humid summers.

The curing of Culatello di Zibello is a cottage industry and it is not mass produced. A treat so precious that finding it even in the Zibello region is not an easy feat.

We were lucky to be invited to taste it at La Buca, in the heart of the small commune of Zibello itself where we enjoyed a long lunch with Culatello in each course.

Trattoria La Buca, ZIBELLO

Miriam Leonardi, landlady and chef, treated us to all the local specialities from luscious home made mostarda, freshly sliced Prosciutto di Parma, chunks of Parmigiano with a drizzle of Aceto Balsamico and, of course, Culatello from their own prized production.

A thin slice of Culatello on rustic bread with a home-made Mostarda di Pere – thickly cut slices of pear preserved in syrup and mustard oil was delicious, but it was an unexpected treat to have it in Miriam's tagliatelle fatte in Casa con Culatello (home made tagliatelle with wafer thin Culatello). The pasta was perfectly cooked with what we believed was the lightest butter dressing we'd ever tasted and the succulent shreds of Culatello were all adorned with just enough Parmigiano.

It was a sublime dish, perfectly portioned.

The meal was accompanied by magnums of Lambrusco Reggiano, DOC, 2005, Medici Ermete, produced by our old friend Alberto at Tenuta La Rampata, Reggio Emilia.

This was Lambrusco as it should be – dry but fruity at the same time, soft, fresh, lively and pleasantly harmonious. There was an understated elegance to this wine which manifested itself on the palate. It was representative of its terroir, respectful of its origins and bursting with Emilia-Romagna's charm.

LASAGNE

Serves six people

Lasagne is a long time favourite at the restaurant, and has featured on the menu since we opened in 1996.

My granny was famous for her lasagne, which became her signature dish. The ingredients she used are a little different to those most British people are accustomed to, and the finished dish is a little drier.

Nonna used to take four hours to make the ragu, a mixture of veal, pork and pork sausage. Oils are released by the meats as they slowly cook, and as children at home we used to love dipping bread into it as it cooked. The oil was so flavoursome! Her original recipe is featured on page 153.

In true Italian tradition our recipe at the restaurant has been adapted over the years.

For the ragu

2kg beef mince	2kg pork mince

For the soffritto, mince:

2 onions	2 carrots
2 sticks of celery	
4 cloves crushed garlic	100g chopped marjoram
250g chopped pancetta (using the rind as a bouquet garni)	
½ bottle white wine	½ltr milk
2ltr Sugo (See page 134)	2 grated nutmegs

In a heavy saucepan seal the mince in olive oil until golden brown, strain off excess oil - remove and set to one side.
Pour the white wine into the heavy saucepan to release the meaty flavours. Reduce by half.
In a separate pan sweat the soffritto, garlic, marjoram, and pancetta until soft.
Add the mince and soffritto together with the other wet ingredients, season with salt, pepper & nutmeg. Bring to the boil, turn to simmer & cook out for 2-3 hours skimming the pot regularly.

For the besciamella

1.2ltr milk	60g unsalted butter
60g plain flour	1 onion
2 fresh bay leaves	2 cloves
½ grated nutmeg	salt & pepper

Place the milk, onion, nutmeg clove & bayleaf in a heavy bottomed pan & gently bring to the boil. Set aside.
In a separate suitable pan, melt the butter then add the flour, stir briskly until a paste is formed.
Add the milk mix to the butter mix a ¼ at a time stirring continuously to beat out any lumps, when all the milk is added, turn the gas down to simmer & cook for a further 2-3 minutes to produce a glossy sauce.

Assembling the lasagne:

Ladle a thin layer of besciamella on a large square deep oven tray.
Layer on top the pasta sheets to cover.
Add a layer of ragu, then fresh pasta, then ragu again, layer of fresh pasta and finish off with besciamella.
Sprinkle with parmesan between the layers and on top.
Bake in the oven for 30-45 minutes until crispy on top and the pasta has cooked.

Pasta E FAGIOLI

Bean and pasta soup – Serves four people

Ingredients

300g Borlotti beans
(soak overnight in 3ltr of water with a
pinch of bicarbonate soda)
2 bay leaves
1 sprig of thyme
1 garlic clove (whole)

2 carrots (1cm dice)
6 red onions (1cm dice)
3 sticks of celery (1cm dice)
250g diced pancetta
4 cloves garlic (chopped)
3 large sprigs of rosemary
(finely chopped)
2 dried chillies
1ltr Sugo (see recipe on page 134)
Maltagliati pasta

Method

Rinse off the soaked beans.

Place in a pan with 2 bay leaves, 1 sprig of thyme and 1 garlic clove

Cover with water and bring to boil.

The starch from the beans will form a foam on the top of the water, skim this off with a ladle.

Turn down to simmer & cook the beans until tender, it's important at this stage not to salt your beans or they will become tough.

Meanwhile, sweat off the carrot, onion, celery, pancetta, rosemary, garlic & dried chilli until very soft.

When the borlotti beans are cooked, remove half of them & place in with the vegetable mix.

Push the remainder through a fine sieve then add to the vegetable mix. Pour in the Sugo & bring to the boil.

Add some of the cooking water from the beans to create the consistency required, it should remain quite thick.

Season to taste.

Finally add the maltagliati until cooked and finish with good olive oil & shaved parmesan.

Gian with Italian aunties Gabby and Lidia

Trattoria "La Buca"

43010 Zibello
Parma
Tel. 0039 (0)524 99214
info@trattorialabuca.com
www.trattorialabuca.com

A small country restaurant in the heart of Zibello that cures its own Culatello. We had the five course meal with Culatello in every course, highly recommended – the fresh pastas are also especially good.
Their stock of Levi Grappa's is truely amazing, you'll need one after a lunch like this!

Galleria Ferrari

Via Dino Ferrari, 43
Maranello,
Near Modena, Emilia-Romagna
Tel. 0039 (0)536 949713
galleria@ferrari.it
www.galleria.ferrari.com

This is the exhibition centre for Ferrari, the race track is nearby. As a kid my grandad used to take me here and we used to watch the Ferraris on the test track – being close to the track with the scent of burning rubber and the high-pitched engines racing by, it still rings in my ears.

Medici Ermete & Figli S.r.l.

Via Newton, 13 - 42040 Gaida – Reggio Emilia
Tel. 0039 (0)522 942135
medici@medici.it
www.medici.it

Alberto now runs the business. They produce not only great wines, but traditional balasmic vinegar – Alberto showed us great hospitality sharing his secrets and passion for foods of the area. Well worth a visit to the cantina to experience the wines first hand – I'd recommend trying his single vineyard Concerto Lambrusco with the bolitto misto, a local delicacy.

the answer is in
TORINO

Looking back it was inevitable that I would end up in the restaurant business, yet my first experience of a professional kitchen came by chance.

When I was 14 a friend was working in a local hotel and one day he called me for help. The kitchen was short of a pot washer and they wondered if I fancied a part-time job.

It was the start of a career that saw me move into the Italian restaurant scene firstly at the Montgomery Hotel, then the Pizzeria San Remo and eventually to my mother's restaurant La Romantica.

There I progressed from pot washing to making dough and prepping before I eventually became head chef while studying for a Master's degree in Sports Medicine and Sports Science.

By this time my old school friend Maurizio had gone to catering college and on to do his stages in Austria,

Switzerland and Italy. Maurizio's father, Moreno Mori, was a pioneer of the Italian restaurant trade in Sheffield. His son was keen to get the formal training required to follow into the profession.

We kept in touch and vowed that one day we would go into business together.

Even as late as the 1990s the Sheffield Italian restaurant and café scene reflected British tastes and there was nothing of the authentic foods we had seen on our trips to Italy.

There was something missing in the city and there seemed to be an opportunity. Then one day I drove down Hickmott Road and the butcher's shop on the corner was for sale. It seemed like a really good spot and as soon as I walked inside I knew what I wanted to do. Spurred on by my wife Melanie, who encouraged me all the way, I picked up the phone…

I called Maurizio in Montecatini and told him our dream for a coffee bar with a deli and a small restaurant offering Sheffield its first authentic taste of Italy was about to become reality and the idea of Nonna's was born.

LATTE
PARZIALMENTE SCREMATO

OLIO DI SEMI

VENDITA DI CARNI FRESCHE
S U I N E

Bruno Dalmazio and Silvia Gallucci

We acquired the premises and simply decided to go for it. We had no business plan, just a driving ambition to create something different.

Our upbringing and backgrounds meant we knew Italian products inside out, but we soon discovered that it was virtually impossible to get hold of them in the UK. We had a lot of shelves to fill in our new little deli and the perfect corner that was going to be the coffee bar. But where were we going to get the products to fill the shelves and where in the world were we going to get our espresso machine?

The answer soon dawned on us. We would have to go to Italy and get them!

We hired a van, borrowed £5,000 in cash and headed off. The first stop was Turin and the headquarters of the mighty Lavazza empire. We knew that the company would help fit out the coffee bar if we used their coffee. We reached the office, changed into suits in the back of the van and knocked on the door. I will never forget their reaction. They simply couldn't understand why two young guys would drive in a van from the UK to talk to them without even making an appointment. But the tactic worked. We met the export director and told him our plans. Italians warm to people when they meet face to face and from that initial meeting we cut the ice and were introduced to the Lavazza UK agent. A deal was struck and our coffee bar was destined to become the real thing.

With success under our belts we went on a tour stocking up the van with all kinds of products for the deli. We wanted to ensure we could offer an authentic taste of Italy, largely from artisan producers, so we could go home and introduce Sheffield folk to flavours and experiences they had never encountered before.

Maurizio remembered buying a 100-year-old barrel for next to nothing and coming across Caparsini Chianti Classico, which we enjoyed so much we decided to have it on our first wine list at Nonna's. We even used a map of the vineyard as table mats.

It was during this trip that we met Bruno Dalmazio, a man who has continued to play a large part in our story over the years as Nonna's has developed.

Bruno is one of our major suppliers who has helped develop Nonna's branded products.

Thanks to Bruno and also our own hunting for authentic foods and wines we soon spent our £5,000, had filled the van and were heading back home to prepare to launch our business.

"A deal was struck and our coffee bar

was destined to become the real thing."

a taste of Italy
PASTA

No food has a national identity as strong as pasta and children across the world soon get to know its country of origin.

In its simplest form, it is made from a mixture of flour and water, but it often has eggs and other ingredients such as spinach, as in Nonna's original lasagne.

It also comes in all shapes and sizes and can be fresh or dried, both of which can be very good.

The best known pasta is spaghetti but there are scores of others such as cannelloni, penne, fusilli, linguine, orecchiette, ravioli, tortellini and rigatoni.

Some have a romantic legend attached, as in tortellini, which is said to have been inspired by Venus' navel.

It is testimony to the skills of the traditional pasta makers that few people even attempt to make their own and most is bought in a packet.

If you can't make your own but want to taste the real thing you should head to our Cucina. At Nonna's we make all our own pasta for use in the restaurant and we sell fresh varieties each day in the Cucina for people to take home. We have developed gluten free versions as well.

Many sauces have evolved over the years to accompany pasta, and like the pasta shapes themselves, most have evolved from Italy's distinct regions.

In Italy the use of sauce is often to lightly dress the pasta, unlike the tradition in Britain which is to add it in much larger quantities.

Italians favour it al dente, that is with a bit of bite, although some regions seem to have different ideas on exactly how firm it should be. Salt is always added to the cooking pan, but olive oil is added only after it has been put on the plate.

Ristorante LA PINETA

Sandro Piattelli from La Baita restaurant (see page 148) introduced us to this great find.

It's in a unique spot, difficult to get to, though once there owner Luciano Zazzeri will make you feel at home, personally taking your order as you gaze out to sea.

La Pineta is a small restaurant, basically a beach shack, but don't be put off by the exterior. Once inside you'll find an elegant dining area with blue fittings, dark wood cupboards and chairs with tables set with spotless white linen and full silver cutlery.

Luciano is a natural chef, from a family of fishermen – in fact his brothers still supply the seafood to the restaurant. In his hands La Pineta has become one of the most renowned seafood restaurants in Tuscany.

Luciano's experience as a fisherman and his knowledge of fish has allowed his creativity to flourish. He is always looking to develop new recipes which are full of fantasy but always based on fresh, mostly local fish, cooked in such a way to keep the natural flavours alive. Somehow he manages to re-interpret recipes of the local and Tuscan tradition, while introducing subtle new ingredients and his original ideas.

The wine list is world class. It's obviously dominated by whites to match the fish, and all of Italy's regions are well represented. But there is a fantastic collection of reds mainly from Tuscany, including the famous Sassicaia and Ornellaia, and others from Piedmont, Veneto and Trentino.

Luciano and La Pineta have received many accolades including a Michelin star but the approach and setting keeps the atmosphere relaxed.

Cacciucco
ALLA LIVORNESE

Livornese Fish Stew – Serves four people

Ingredients

(700g) of mixed fish, use whatever is in season, inexpensive: sole, mullet, catfish, dogfish, goby, squid, octopus, fresh shellfish, shrimp.

Chop the large fish & keep the small ones whole.

1 onion (medium dice)

2 cloves garlic (whole)

1 small bunch of parsley (roughly chopped)

3 tbsp olive oil

(500g) ripe plum tomatoes, blanched and peeled then diced

3 tbsp red wine vinegar

6 tbsp water

For the Seasoning

2 dried chillies

toasted Tuscan bread rubbed liberally with garlic

Method

Sauté the onion, parsley, and garlic in the olive oil in a deep bottomed pan.

Once the onion is cooked, stir in the plum tomatoes & season the mixture to taste.

This dish can take a bit of spice so don't be scared with the chilli.

When the tomatoes are cooked, stir in the water & vinegar, simmer for a few more minutes then remove the garlic.

Blend the sauce & return it to the heat.

Add the chopped fish.

Simmer for 10-15 minutes until the fish is just coming off the bone.

Add a splash more of olive oil & check the seasoning.

Meanwhile toast several slices of Tuscan bread & rub them with a clove of garlic.

Once the stew is done, line the bottom of the bowl with the toasted bread, ladle the Cacciucco over them & serve.

Spaghetti alle VONGOLE

Spaghetti with clams - Serves four people

Ingredients

250g unsalted butter (soft)
zest & juice of 3 lemons
2 fresh red chillies (chopped)
1 dried chilli (crushed)
1 small bunch parsley (chopped)

Mix the above ingredients together until they are evenly blended. Set aside.

1kg surf clams
1 small glass of white wine

Method

Place a heavy bottomed saucepan on the stove and wait until it is red hot (smoking).
Put the clams in the pan with the wine, place a lid on top & steam open the clams.
Add the combined butter mixture to the clams & combine together.
Season with salt and pepper.

Meanwhile take 300g of spaghetti & cook in boiling water, salted for 6-8 minutes.
When cooked, strain off & toss through the clams.
Tip:- You shouldn't add parmesan cheese to seafood dishes.

L to R: Gian Bohan, award-winning Chianina cattle breeder Fosco Mecherini & Luciano Zazzeri, chef/proprietor of Ristorante La Pineta

Bruno Dalmazio
BD ENOTECA s.r.l.
via Traversa dei Monti, 214
53024 MONTALCINO (SI)
Tel. 0039 (0)577 849019/849083
www.dalmazio.com

We've known Bruno for over 12 years, since our initial search for products for the deli. Like ours, Bruno's business has expanded over the years and now his showcase store is halfway up the hill to Montalcino.
On display is a fantastic array of wines and food products which you are able to taste. Coincidentally, Bruno's niece Silvia worked at Nonna's while studying in England. You may even see some of Nonna's products on the shelves.

Ristorante La Pineta
Via dei Cavalleggeri Nord, 27
57020 Marina di Bibbona
Livorno
Tel. 0039 (0)586 600016
Closed: Oct – Nov 10; Mon, Tues lunch

One of Tuscany's finest restaurants. Tucked away on the beach near Marina di Bibbona, I would recommend booking as La Pineta is extremely popular, and for good reason!

Mercato Ittico di Livorno
Via Padre G.B.Saglietto 8, 57100 Livorno
Tel. 0039 (0)586 895582
www.mercatoitticolivorno.it more information on www.comune.livorno.it

Markets in Italy always hold a special place for me, and this is certainly no exception. With it being coastal the fish displays are mind boggling, watching the skilled fishmongers at work, strike up a conversation on the ingredients of Cacciucco, the local fish stew, and you will have a lively heated debate on your hands of which fish is best to use.

CHAPTER three

Something lucky or JUST PLAIN FISHY

With plentiful supplies for the deli and the promise of the coffee shop being adorned with Lavazza logos, it was time to get to work.

Although we had no business plans or projections at the time there was no doubt what our new venture would be named.

Nonna had been one of the biggest influences in my life and naming it after her seemed the obvious choice, although there were plenty of people around at the time who thought we were making a mistake.

Maurizio's parents, Moreno and Leda were great sounding boards. They were well-known on the Italian restaurant scene in Sheffield before us, running such places as the Victoria Wine Bar, the Dam House restaurant and Pizzeria Giovanni.

Maurizio has always said that his father has been the greatest influence on his life and if we ever needed advice we knew he was always just a phone call away in Montecatini. He was like the man above, keeping an eye on us and reeling us back in if we got too carried away in our early excitement.

In June 1996 Nonna herself cut the ribbon and we opened for the first time. It was a memorable day – it had started with a surprise "present" of a fish being pushed through the letterbox. To this day we don't know who did it or its significance. Was it a good luck token or a Sicilian-style warning?

Our families had all helped out, Granny had given us her recipes, her old rolling pin and treasured photographs were hanging on the wall.

From the very start we decided to stick to our principles. It was an authentic taste of Italy in Sheffield and it was more than just the food.

We didn't put stools at the bar because we wanted people to stand Italian style, with a coffee and a cornetto, a bread shaped like the French croissant, reading La Gazzetta dello Sport or looking at Rai Uno on Italian TV.

We were serving rich, strong arabica coffee from our Gaggia machine and we all had to learn how to make decent Italian coffee with proper crema and properly steamed milk. Wisely, Maurizio invited his friends Roberto and Danilla Innocenti to come over from Montecatini for the opening. Roberto is an expert barista and he guided us through the steaming of milk. We tried all sorts of milk to ensure we got the creamy consistency we needed. On day one we sold 400 cappuccinos and the couple have remained great friends.

Preparing food for the opening was also a nerve wracking experience and we decided to try and test everything to make sure we had got things just right.

The chefs were working through the night to perfect recipes and Maurizio even had to go to his mother's flat to raid her kitchen for the correct pans to make ragu.

We used our little deli to showcase great Italian products such as salamis, mortadella, Parma ham, olive oils, balsamic vinegars and stunning Italian wines.

From the word go we were busy; people had seen nothing like it before in Sheffield, and it is a trend that has thankfully continued.

People told us Nonna's had a great atmosphere which made people think they were in Italy; that was the biggest compliment they could have paid us.

Our original plan was for Maurizio and me to do everything, but by the end of the second week we had employed five waitresses including a girl who had knocked on the door and asked if she could have a job. Her name was Patrizia, and now she's Maurizio's wife!

It was a steep learning curve and we had to pick things up quickly but we had lots of passion and great authentic products.

Our families were a great help and I had the support of my wife Melanie, who had to put up with my long hours at work.

As we were originally licensed until just 6pm, we started by serving good, simple, honest food – cucina povera, or poor man's food, such as bruschetta, crostini and simple dishes like pappa al pomodoro, which uses kitchen leftovers to great effect.

They were good wholesome meals, true to our philosophy of letting the produce express themselves to show the quality of the ingredients.

Our menus have changed over the years as our knowledge and love of food has developed.

We have often wondered why it worked so well from the start. Perhaps it was because people could come in for coffee, experience the atmosphere, stay for lunch, buy something to take home for dinner and buy niche wines, many of them not found elsewhere in Sheffield, if not the UK.

It was a busy job but being in Nonna's became part of our lives. Even when we were not working we would come to eat, taste the wine and our enthusiasm blossomed. You never stop learning about good food and wine and we had created a culinary font of knowledge that was our own.

We still have our first evening menu and looking at it now it still looks good, a reflection on good ingredients served simply.

These days our menu is more complex and we are a well-oiled business with proper projections, a website, outside catering and the highly popular and regular gatherings of our food and wine club, hosted by some of the biggest names in the business.

But we have remained true to our original aims. Now we make as many items as we can, including the breads, pasta, biscuits and ice cream.

Over the years we expanded as adjoining properties became available and the licensing laws were relaxed.

We launched our first Italian-style wine bar, an enoteca, after acquiring the newsagent's next door and we were able to put more dinner tables in the front.

In 2005 we expanded again and opened the bar and later the Cucina on Hickmott Road in order to develop our limited kitchen space and to make more of our in-house products.

cultura del CAFFÈ

Italians have been drinking great coffee from year dot and it is an indelible part of their culture. It was of course a different experience in England where a cup of tea was usually favoured.

When we opened, people thought we had created the new wheel. Customers were thrilled by the hissing and gurgling of the espresso machine in action and the banging and rattling of Maurizio or myself preparing fresh coffees.

We wanted the genuine article and we were convinced it would take off in the heart of Ecclesall Road. That meant we needed a little bar area with no seats – Italians like to pop in for a quick coffee and a chat before making off on their business.

Italians and their coffee cannot be parted and the art of making good coffee, and the way it is taken is a ritual that is a deep-seated way of life in all parts of Italy.

Maurizio tells great stories of Italian coffee culture, many passed down from his parents, who eventually returned to live in Montecatini. Maurizio has introduced me to many places from his side of Tuscany, including Bar Giovannini in Montecatini Terme, one of the best coffee bars I've ever seen. Here they make great little cakes and pastries – pasticini – all on show in a mouth watering window display.

Italians regard a trip for a coffee as an essential daily ritual that they will repeat through the day. Coffee shops are known as bars and they are community meeting places where people will gather to argue about football and politics on the way to work, at lunchtime, on the way home and whenever during the day they can make it.

Cappuccino is served only in the morning, never after lunch and the milk is never boiled. It is heated lukewarm so it blends with the coffee crema. Unlike the popular habit here, in Italy cappuccinos rarely have chocolate on top of the foam.

Often Italians have a glass of sparkling water before an espresso as it agitates the taste buds and adds to the appreciation of the coffee.

bar pasticceria GIOVANNINI

Giovannini's is an iconic coffee bar which is currently celebrating its 80th year.

It epitomises everything that a traditional Italian coffee bar should be. In the morning by 11am the place is buzzing with all sorts of people; well-heeled bankers and their customers enjoying an espresso and little choux pastry cakes called bignè, and others popping in to buy cakes to take away.

Giovannini's is famous for its little quirks. It's a place where you pay for your coffee first and you are given a little ticket to give to the barista. My wife Melanie loves it – she reckons it's the only place in the world where she gets four grown men making her a coffee – one calling the order, another arranging the saucers while two others are making the coffee and frothing the milk. What a contrast to the regimented American-style coffee places we have back home, which will remain nameless!

By early evening it takes on a different guise as Italians dress in their finest and descend on the town centre to enjoy the traditional pastime of La Passeggiata – the evening stroll. Part of this involves the famous aperitivo culture where folk will pop into their favourite bars to enjoy an aperitivi with complimentary stuzzichini at the counter.

All bars in Italy do this at different levels – Giovannini's is a particularly stylish place – and the aperitivo culture sums up the differences between the Italians and the British. It's not a question of standing all night at the bar eating all the nibbles and drinking as much as you can; in Italy it is about having one or two aperitivi before moving on for dinner.

Giovannini's does this so well, and it is something we have successfully emulated at Nonna's where our early evening aperitivi hour and complimentary stuzzichini have proved a great success.

PASTICCERIA
GIOVANNINI
MONTECATINI TERME
PASTICCERIA
GIOVANNINI
MONTECATINI TERME
PASTICCERIA
GIOVANNINI
MONTECATINI TERME

Almond
CANTUCCINI BISCUITS

Makes 50 small biscuits

Ingredients

325g "00" flour

300g caster sugar

1 ½ tsp baking powder

½ tsp ground cinnamon

½ tsp salt

325g whole blanched almonds

3 large free-range eggs

1 vanilla pod split in half & seeds removed

1 tsp vanilla extract

Method

Line 2 baking sheets with greaseproof paper.

Roughly crush around a third of the almonds.

In a bowl combine the flour, sugar, baking powder, cinnamon and salt. Stir together.

Add all of the nuts.

In another bowl whisk the eggs & vanilla.

Add the wet dough.

Turn out onto a floured work surface, divide in half.

Roll each half under the palms of your hands into a cylinder shape, place the logs onto the baking sheet.

Gently press down to flatten slightly.

Bake for 25-35 minutes until the logs have risen & spread to double in size, they are done when firm to touch.

Remove to cooling wire to chill.

When chilled slice on the diagonal into $^1/_4$" thick slices.

Back into the oven for an extra 10-15 minutes until golden brown.

Leave to chill.

Store in a biscuit tin or a jar – the biscuits will keep for up to a week.

Ideal to serve with a nice pannacotta or just for dunking in a caffè latte or Vin Santo.

Stuzzichini APERITIVI BITES

Aperitivi time in Milan and northern Italy is sacred. With your Campari and soda or bellini or spritz (a wine spritzer served in Veneto with a dash of Aperol), Italians offer a range of titillating "stuzzichini" as accompaniment.

Here are some delicious easy recipes for aperitivo time.

POMODORINI RIPIENI

Small tomatoes (salad tomatoes will be fine but you can make even more with cherry tomatoes)

50g tuna in olive oil

3 green olives

6 capers

1tbsp mayonnaise

Cut the top of the tomato, spoon out contents and de-seed. Salt lightly and place on a plate to allow remaining water content to drain. De-salt the capers by washing them in water – drain well.

Chop the olives roughly.

Drain the oil from the tuna and place in a bowl – add the capers, olives and a heaped spoon of mayonnaise, mix well.

Drain any excess water from the tomatoes and stuff them with the tuna mixture.

Serve.

ROMBI DI POLENTA AL FORMAGGIO

250g polenta flour

1ltr water

salt

200g taleggio (or parmesan or dolcelatte or montasio) (or why not all four)

In a wide deep pan (if you have a copper one even better) add the water and a heap table spoon of salt. (Not too much as you will be adding cheese which will add a lot of flavour). When it comes to a boil, slowly add the polenta flour, (you don't want the pot to stop boiling), stirring constantly with a wooden spoon to keep lumps from forming.

Continue stirring, in the same direction, as the mixture thickens, for about a half an hour.

5 minutes before it's done add the taleggio and allow it to melt.

The polenta is done when it peels easily off the sides of the pot.

Spread it out to cool in a 1cm deep dish. Once cold, cut into diamond shapes and serve.

You can also make "crostini of polenta" by topping the squares with good pan-fried sliced sausage or a slice of Coppa, Speck or Salami.

CROSTINI CON SALSICCIA & STRACCHINO CHEESE

3 salsicce (fresh Italian pork sausages)

300g stracchino cheese (a sharp flavoured creamy, spreading cheese)

12 slices unsalted Focaccia bread

Remove the skin from the sausages; place the meat in a large bowl and combine with the stracchino, mixing them together well.

Cut a dozen or so slices of bread about a centimetre thick and put in the grill for approx. five minutes, until crisp on both sides.

Remove from the grill and allow to cool.

Spread some of the mixture on each slice.

Put back in under the grill for a few more minutes and serve the crostini hot.

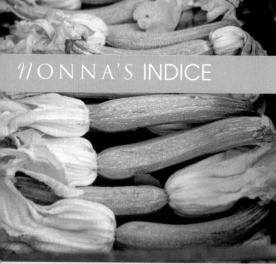

Pasticceria Giovannini,

Corso Matteotti, 4
Montecatini Terme (PT)
Tel. 0039 (0)572 78958
gemmagiovannini@virgilio.it

For me the day starts once I've had a cappuccino and a panino of Parma ham, artichoke puree in fresh poppy seed bread. Their selection of cakes and snacks is mouthwatering, you'll often see the well-heeled locals taking away the prettily wrapped up Giovannini packages.

Vecchia Trattoria Buralli

Piazza S. Agostino, 10
55100 - Lucca (LU)
Tel. 0039 (0)583 950611

With the centre of Lucca being a tourist haven it's hard to find a good local restaurant. Trattoria Buralli is off the tourist trails with an outside terrace. They offer great set menu specials each day. Try the Zuppa di Farro and the local Colline Lucchesi wines.

Ristorante Egisto

Piazza C. Battisti 13,
Montecatini Terme (PT)
Tel. 0039 (0)572 78413
www.egisto.it

Trendy place to be seen in the heart of Montecatini. Serves a variety of pizza, pasta and grills all done with flair. Hustle and bustle but don your best togs to be seen.

Gallo Pizzeria

Via del Gallo, 148
Pieve a Nievole,
51016 – Montecatini Terme (PT)
Tel. 0039 (0)572 80335

Just outside Montecatini in a suburban area, but don't be fooled this unassuming place serves the best pizza in the area. Traditional wood burning oven, the pizza for me, when in season, is Porcini mushroom and Stracchino cheese. They also have a good antipasti buffet.

CHAPTER four

Road to BOLGHERI

In common with most people with an Italian background, I was introduced to the pleasures of the grape at a relatively early age.

My parents used to let me drink watered down wine at the dinner table from the age of about 12 and it was the start of a continuing passion and a thirst for knowledge about everything to do with winemaking.

Starting young really helped me to understand about the qualities of wine. Alcohol was secondary to the appreciation of the ancient craft and an understanding of the marriage of food and wine.

From my very first sips I was absorbed by the romance of it all. Since those early days I have been intrigued by the skills of the winemaker's art and fascinated by the many different factors that can make a wine great or indifferent.

My main interest has been in Italian wines. It is amazing that Italy is home to more than 350 grape varieties, offering wines of unique flavours and characteristics. Every day seems to bring a new wine experience and the thrill of unearthing a new unexpected treasure cannot be beaten.

Every time I visit Italy I seem to find something I have not tasted before and it is always an immense joy. I feel as if I'm the first person ever to have tasted it and all I want to do is tell everybody about my new discovery.

We like to think that Nonna's is an ambassador for the alluring qualities of Italian wines. Our list has more than 100 constantly changing choices, representing all the regions. It is an ever-evolving collection, a testimony to our expanding knowledge. We think we have got to know a lot about Italian wines by now, but the fact is we are still continuing to learn all the time, constantly making new discoveries.

Italy enables you to do that. With its great diversity of grape varieties and a multitude of small producers willing to experiment with blends and styles, you are always likely to uncover something different and special if you look hard and know the right people.

Wine production on this small scale produces great individuality. Hand crafted artisan wines, made by dedicated producers determined to retain their unique flavours are a joy to discover. At Nonna's, we are proud to offer the fruits of our adventures to our customers. They are unlikely to find anything like them in the supermarket or in fact in many wine merchants outside Italy.

The joy of wine is that you don't have to drink the very best all the time. Appreciating wine is a sensory experience that is affected by time, place and occasion as much as the quality of the product.

How many times have you tasted and loved a wine on holiday when you are relaxed over a romantic al fresco meal for two, with the sun setting over the horizon, only to find that it doesn't give the same satisfaction when you return home?

This is the hidden sense of wine. Back home it has the same colour, aroma and taste but it has lost something… it's the sense of occasion that's missing. When you enjoyed it on holiday you were in a different world, a world you cannot recreate over your own dinner table or in your lounge sitting in front of the TV.

Different occasions call for different wines. For my 40th birthday party at our Tuscan property Casa di Nonna's, I didn't need an expensive wine – unbottled wine out of a demijohn from down the road in Montecarlo was the right choice for that occasion. A sense of place is important when drinking wine. The long-lasting memories come from the entire experience not just the quality of the wine itself.

Because of my developing knowledge of Italian wine and my understanding that local foods are often best matched by local wines, it seemed Montecarlo wine was the obvious choice for my party. Italians have the expression L'abbinamento – "the match" – which sums up what I mean. The surroundings, the special occasions and the friends around the table enjoying a simple yet delicious meal required L'abbinamento and Montecarlo provided it to perfection.

Another magical moment when the setting, the mood and the wine came together, was just last year at Casa di Nonna's.

Many of our family had been over for the week and as they left for home, my wife Melanie and I were alone to enjoy the final night before we packed up and moved on.

I prepared a typical piatti di mare – a simple yet delicious swordfish dish with capers, lemon rind, lemon juice and olive oil.

We were sitting out enjoying the sunset, Melanie was wondering what had happened to all the wine – well it was the last day and it had all been consumed.

I had a bottle of 1967 Dom Perignon that an uncle in Modena had given me. I'd been saving it to enjoy with what Melanie calls my "wine geek friends" but wine is for the occasion, and this was one of those.

vini e
prodotti
locali

olio di
nostra
produzione

AMABILE

Vin Santo del Nonno

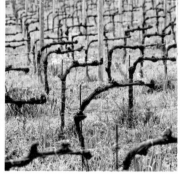

"Every day seems to bring a new wine experience and the thrill of unearthing a new unexpected treasure cannot be beaten."

I chilled it down and popped the cork… it was one of those momentous wine moments I dream about. Perfect company, beautiful surroundings and the wine, which had mellowed slightly to a dark amber colour, but held its lively spritz – it was simply sublime.

Our trips to Italy, in search of the best foods and wines to bring back to Nonna's and to add to our education have unearthed some stunning discoveries, from simple house wines that never get bottled, to world class Barolos and Super Tuscans.

My family are rooted in Modena, in Emilia-Romagna, while Maurizio's folk are from the Montecatini area a little to the west, in Tuscany itself, where we discovered Casa di Nonna's up in the hills.

From the simplicity of the Montecarlo DOC we have discovered many hidden treasures and also tasted some of the world's greatest rated wines at source, often sitting overlooking the vineyards where the grapes grow.

On the west coast, south of Pisa is the Bolgheri wine DOC growing district.

The region's wines had lost their way until the 1950s when Mario Incisa della Rocchetta planted Cabernet Sauvignon cuttings from Chateau Lafite on his vineyard called Sassicaia (stony ground) on his Tenuta San Guido estate.

By the 1960s it was being tasted and enjoyed at wine fairs and suddenly it was a phenomenon.

It is now regarded as arguably Italy's greatest wine and was the catalyst for massive investment in the area in the 1980s by forward-thinking wine makers, frustrated by the restrictions of the DOC regulations. They started making wines, like the Sassicaia estate, using non-indigenous grapes much to the bemusement of the wine regulators. Using grapes such as Cabernet Sauvignon and Merlot, they fell foul of the DOC restrictions and their wines had to be labelled as IGT or Vdt, equivalent to the French Vin de Pays – ordinary country wine.

They were more extraordinary than ordinary and popularly became known as Super Tuscans appreciated the world over for their fantastic quality, great structure and ability to improve with age. These were the wines that well and truly put Italy back on the world map of the highest quality wines, with an investment potential to match the top growth clarets.

My first taste of Sassicaia came just as we got the keys to Casa di Nonna's.

I'm a great believer in marking special occasions with a great wine and we were having dinner at Castello La Torre where we drank Sassicaia, to the delight of the head waiter.

It was an unforgettable occasion marked by the romance of my first taste of a very special bottle of wine.

Since then I have gone on to be an aficionado of the great Sassicaia and have built up a vertical "museum" collection.

We also sell it in Nonna's, where we keep the mark up to a minimum, to allow as many customers as can afford it the opportunity to share our passion of enjoying a special wine, in what we hope they regard as a special place.

I will never forget standing at the bottom of the road to Bolgheri, being swept away by the sight of the very cypress trees that inspired the poet Giosuè Carducci to write "Davanti a San Guido" more than a century before and being totally mesmerised by the great story of how that little area of stony ground started the unstoppable renaissance of top quality Italian wine.

As Melanie often remarks I seem to have a geekish ability to remember where I first tasted the wines I have come to enjoy and share with my friends and customers and I hope that some of the joy I get from researching wines and discovering new flavours is passed down in our enoteca and at the table.

To this day I can remember the Barolo producer whose wines were on the list at my mother's restaurant La Romantica when I was a teenager washing the dishes.

My own journey of discovery of that great, big, robust deep red wine Barolo has since been one of intense pleasure and, as ever, the wine itself has always been an introduction to another great experience.

Martino Maniero introduced me to wine importer Angelo Carne who once took me on a tour of Barolo vineyards just to the south west of his home town, Alba, in the heart of truffle country.

The white Alba truffle is one of the world's most prized delicacies. Gourmets throughout the world eagerly await the season, which runs from October to January, and as supplies dwindle over the years, the prices have rocketed.

We were in Alba with Angelo who took us to the village of Barolo for lunch where we enjoyed fonduta, a creamy mixture of egg, milk and Fontina cheese, with truffle shavings on top. It was so delicious we decided we wanted to buy some truffles to take home.

Truffle hunters – trifolao – are very secretive and go out in hunt of their precious prey at night with their dogs that sniff out the prized subterranean tubers.

Even the process of buying them has an ancient mystique about it, and it is very much a question of being in the know.

Angelo persuaded his father to take us to the market to buy truffles and he showed us what to look for, especially the best colour and scent.

The intense pungent smell of an Alba truffle is amazing; even wrapped correctly in a slightly damp cloth in your pocket the aroma still comes out.

Two years later we returned to the area to buy truffles again and we were mistaken for novice tourists with no idea what we were looking for. We were offered some truffles with hardly any aroma and we turned them down. We had been taught by Angelo's father that we needed to pick out the ones with the overpowering perfume of the woods. In classic Italian fashion the shopkeeper went into his back room and returned with his prized collection. These truffles were out of this world and the whole adventure demonstrated the old fashioned Italian tradition of holding on to the best things you have got for yourself!

The whole of the Barolo area in Piedmont, with its misty rolling hills and steep sided vineyards is magical, and it provides a wonderful change from the heat of the tourist clogged Renaissance cities and seaside resorts.

Touring the area provides so much enjoyment, whatever the weather.

Near Casa di Nonna's is the old town of Vinci, its name made famous as the birthplace of the artist Leonardo. One rainy day I was there visiting the Vinci museum and I popped into a bar for an espresso.

In the back I discovered this fantastic enoteca packed with fantastic bottles at really great prices. What started out as a short coffee break ended up as a full blown four-hour lunch with more than a bottle or two from the back room!

It is discoveries like this that has made me determined to be an ambassador for Italian wines at Nonna's.

We use a couple of specialist suppliers, import directly from a number of Italians we have made friends with over the years, especially Martino Maniero, and even bring in wines from our travels to make sure we have one of the finest selections of Italian wines available in any restaurant in the UK.

The policy is to share our passion and to educate our customers to the great breadth of flavours, and Nonna's regularly stages wine dinners hosted by some of Italy's top producers.

There is no end to the knowledge you can absorb about wine, and enjoying the right wine with the best of foods is one of nature's greatest pleasures.

Our list, which has been praised by Decanter Magazine and the AA Good Food Guide, represents wines from all the wine producing regions of Italy and is ever changing as we unearth the latest treasures. Don't be afraid to try something new, you will not be disappointed!

Aceto Balsamico
DI REGGIO EMILIA

One of the first things we needed to put in the back of our van on our first trip to Italy was balsamic vinegar, a product that was slowly becoming popular in the UK.

It has been made for centuries in Nonna's home town Modena, where, even today, production is in the hands of just 40 families who form the Consorzio, a trade association that ensures the quality of the product.

The dark brown nectar is also made in Emilia-Romagna where it's known as Aceto Balsamico Tradizionale di Reggio Emilia.

We have a good relationship with the Medici Ermete family which supplies our fantastically refreshing and underrated Lambrusco, named Concerto.

Medici Ermete doesn't only make great wines like Concerto, but, in good Emilia-Romagna tradition, they produce their own Aceto Balsamico Tradizionale di Reggio Emilia.

But you are unlikely to have any idea just how much care, attention and hours of painstaking dedication that has gone into making it.

We visited Medici Ermete Acetaia at Tenuta Rampata located in the heart of the Lambrusco Reggiano DOC production zone to discover the labour of love that is behind the real Aceto Balsamico.

The everyday Aceto Balsamico Condimento you buy in the supermarket has got nothing to do with Aceto Balsamico Tradizionale.

Aceto Balsamico Tradizionale producers, like Alberto Medici at Ermete, have to follow the ancient methods of production which entail time, patience and dedication. They also have to adhere to the rules and regulations of the consortium, born to protect and guarantee its quality.

Aceto Balsamico starts with cooked grape must, obtained only from Trebbiano Bianco grapes from vines in the production zone of origin, and aged for a minimum of 12-14 years through a system called "batteria" (five barrels of decreasing volume made with different kinds of woods like cherry, oak and mulberry to name a few). It is a natural process which sees the intervention of man only for the particular decanting. Firstly, the grape must goes through alcoholic fermentation before it can start to acetify – this occurs thanks to the forming of a small eco system of enzymes which allows the must to transform.

Every year, the smallest cask of the "batteria" produces only a few litres of balsamic, which must pass the rigorous scrutiny of the consortium's Master Tasters to be awarded any accreditations. If it has reached the balance of flavours which characterises a true Aceto Balsamico it will be allowed to continue its ageing for up to 30 years (pending further taste tests), receive the "Tradizionale" certification and bottled in the characteristic inverted tulip bottles of 100ml, a symbol of the consortium.

This traditional balsamic is not a cheap commodity, due to the complexity and length of time it takes to produce. Depending on its age, the little 100ml bottle will cost at least 200 euros: the older, the better, the more precious it becomes.

The everyday-use Aceto is readily available and considerably cheaper. It is usually bottled before the minimum 12 years requirement by speeding up the acetification mechanically (and yes, if it says Aceto Balsamico aged for seven years, it isn't actually Aceto Balsamico). It is made with both white and red grapes not from the provinces of Modena or Reggio Emilia; colourants and flavourings may be added to imitate the colour and taste.

Alberto offered us a sample of his 18 years (red label), 25 years (silver label) and 30 years (gold label) Aceto Balsamico Tradizionale di Reggio Emilia DOP, Tenuta Rampata, Medici Ermete. Immediately, with the youngest you get taste buds working you didn't know you had. Dark, brown caramel-like drops bursting with scents of precious woods, like cherry, oak and mulberry. With age it becomes even denser and sweeter to a syrup-like consistency.

A few drops are all it takes: these vinegars are not made to be squandered but rather, much like a good wine, to be enjoyed slowly and with complementary ingredients. The love affair with Parmigiano Reggiano, for instance, is a match made in culinary heaven. For a more unusual combination, we were advised to try a few drops of the older ones on vanilla ice cream.

The flavour, perfume, colour and density of a Balsamico Tradizionale are unequivocally inimitable; they tell the story of its makers and of its land through time and accompany, without being second to none, all the other regional specialities. This heritage cannot be manufactured.

the wines of MONTECARLO DOC

Montecarlo is situated in the province of Lucca and used to be called Coste di Vivinaia derived from the ancient Roman Via Vinaria, the Wine Way, that passed through it. The region is blessed with pretty hills, cultivated for centuries with vines and olive groves.

Montecarlo is renowned both for its beautiful location and the production of one of the two prominent DOC wine zones around Lucca, alongside Colli Lucchesi DOC.

Its wines have particular qualities as Montecarlo was the first in Tuscany to adopt foreign varietals alongside the three main indigenous grapes of Trebbiano, Sangiovese and Canaiolo.

Montecarlo DOC makes only a bianco and a rosso and the white is generally regarded as being the best.

The main white wine variety is Trebbiano, but a host of other grapes are allowed including Pinot Bianco, Pinot Grigio, Roussanne, Sauvignon Blanc, Semillon, and Vermentino. The red wine grapes are mainly Sangiovese, but also Canaiolo, Cilegiolo, Colorino, Malvasia, and Syrah.

In the first week of September each year there is the annual fair and market of Montecarlo and Colline Lucchesi DOC.

Zuppa INGLESE

Serves eight

This strange sounding dessert was one my Nonna made for us as children. It's like an Italian version of Sherry trifle.

Ingredients

for the sponge
85g sugar
3 eggs
85g flour
35g melted butter

cherry pureé

fruit liqueur

pistachio nuts

for the milk and honey custard
2 eggs
50g sugar
40g corn flour
250ml milk
200ml condensed milk
200ml evaporated milk
honey to taste

Method

How to make the sponge:

In a large bowl whisk together the sugar and the eggs.

Place over hot water and whisk the mixture until it doubles in size – take off the heat and whisk for a further few minutes – this will prevent it from curdling.

To the mixture now add the sieved flour and the melted butter – fold in well.

Pre-heat the oven at 180°c – place the sponge onto a lined baking tray and bake for 20 minutes.

Leave to cool before cutting into rings.

In the meantime, make your custard:

In a pan heat the evaporated milk.

Whisk together the eggs, sugar and corn flour.

When the evaporated milk is hot, pour onto the mixture and whisk over a bain-marie.

Add the condensed milk and keep whisking over the bain-marie until it begins to thicken.

Take off the heat.

At this point dip the cool round sponge into the cherry pureé and liqueur and place in your round serving glass (you can use any fruit liqueur and pureé you prefer).

Start layering with a piece of sponge, custard, pistachio pureé (or simply sprinkle crushed pistachios) until you reach the end of the glass.

Lingue DI SALE

Ingredients

500ml of sparkling water

200g "00" flour

1 tsp salt

½ tsp crushed black pepper

100ml olive oil

3 sprigs of rosemary removed from stalk (finely chopped)

sea salt

Method

Pre-heat the oven to 180°c.

Whisk the water, flour, salt, pepper & ½ the olive oil to form a batter – it should resemble the consistency of a pancake/Yorkshire pudding batter.

If the mixture is a little thin add a little more flour – if too thick add more water.

Line a baking sheet in grease proof paper, pour a thin layer of the mixture on to the grease proof, put in the oven and cook until golden brown (about 10 minutes).

Just before you take it out of the oven, sprinkle with the chopped rosemary & sea salt, drizzle with olive oil & leave to chill.

Serve with cheeses instead of crackers or with a plate of antipasti cured meats, such as proscuitto San Daniele or lardo di Colonnata.

Da Caino

DA CAINO Via Canonica, 3 – 58014 Montemerano(GR)
Tel. 0039 (0)564 602817
info@dacaino.it or dacaino@relaischateaux.com
www.dacaino.it
Gian Paolo from Poggio Argentario invited us to lunch at Da Caino where he was showcasing his wines.
It's in a small village located in the middle of nowhere.
Da Caino offers Michelin rated food.
Ask them to show you their incredible wine cellars, which run four floors under the hillside and house, it's one of Italy's greatest collections.

Enoteca Grandi Vini Alba

Via Vittorio Emanuele II, 1/A – 12051 Alba CN
Tel. 0039 (0)173 361204
enoteca@grandivinialba.com
www.grandivinialba.com
Alba is a wonderful small town with its roots deep in the traditions of wine and truffles. This small enoteca in the heart of the centro storico has an astonishing array of Barolos and Barbarescos streching back over many fine vintages.

Le Vigne di Cà Nova Srl

Loc Cascina Ca' Nova 1
12050 Roddino (CN)
Tel. 0039 (0)173 794247
canova@vignedicanova.com
www.vignedicanova.com
My good friend Luca from Passione Vini escorted me to this small producer in the heart of the Barolo/Barbaresco area. They harvest two single vineyard Barbaresco's from sites next to the winery. This is how wine making should be, 3,000-5,000 bottles produced in the traditional manner offering outstanding quality and price. They now feature on our wine list.

Tenuta San Guido

Loc. Capanne, 27
57020, Bolgheri (LI)
Tel. 0039 (0)565 762003
www.sassicaia.com
The home of the famous Sassicaia, this is the mecca for the Italian wine renaissance. Based at the foot of the famous undulating Bolgheri road, a great area to explore with so many famous wine houes in a small area, like visiting the first grapes in Bordeaux.

Marinated
Mushrooms
small £2.00
large £4.00

Sundried Plum
Tomatoes
small £2.00
large £6.00

small shop MENTALITY

Nonna's Cucina was a natural progression from our in-store deli and it symbolises our passionate view that people must get back to real shopping.

In Italy they have a "small shop" mentality where it's not unusual for people to do their food shopping on a daily basis.

Yes, they have supermarkets, but Italians crave quality, freshness and above all they savour local regional dishes.

The Italians are really excited about their food. We have always said to people that if they want to start a conversation with a stranger in Italy, then start talking about food.

Food shopping is so different there. Go into a little deli in Bologna for example and ask for some mortadella with pistachio and freshly baked artisan bread. It's poles apart from going to a supermarket for a sandwich.

I guess the seed of my belief in the value of small specialist shops was sewn from my childhood visits to my granny's deli in Modena. She was part of the community there. Everybody would know each others names and they would call in each morning for bread and perhaps a little cheese, Parma ham and pasta.

Shopping for food in Italy is a ritual. People have a good look around for the best seasonal, regional produce and cook according to the best raw ingredients.

Our Cucina aims to replicate the Italian shopping experience.

We bake our own bread daily, prepare freshly-made pastas such as fettuccine, pappardelle and ravioli and we make our own ice cream.

The deli counter serves Italian cured meats and we have our own labeled olive oil, sourced from Puglia.

There is also an enoteca with more than 100 Italian wines.

Olio D'OLIVA

I have a memory etched in my mind of the time I went to Puglia and witnessed a group of old men at Bari harbour enjoying a simple feast of sea urchins. The creatures had been cut in half and the sight of their spikes still moving as if they were trying to protect themselves told of their freshness.

The men were scooping out the bright orange flesh with rustic bread, drizzled with local olive oil.

Puglia is Italy's garden of produce. It supplies so much olive oil, wine, nuts and apricots it's simply great to see.

We were in Puglia to visit olive oil producer Giuseppe Rubini, father of Nonna's wine waiter Domenico Rubini and his family. We toured his groves in a valley blanketed in olive trees, their silvery leaves shimmering like the Adriatic beyond, as his parents prepared us a typical Puglian lunch.

Giuseppe's olive oil is amazing; it's a blend of oils from two olive varieties, Cima di Bitonto and Coratina; the first providing the sweetness necessary to harmonise the marked fragrance of the oil provided by the second olive.

The oil has a fruity flavour with notes of sweet almonds and the fragrance and freshness of ripe and healthy olives. Once picked the olives are immediately taken to the mill in jute sacks or baskets in order to allow a constant circulation of air and to ensure they remain fresh and healthy until they are milled.

Giuseppe revealed the incredible labour of love he puts in to produce this spicy, delicious oil.

We knew straight away that this was the oil we wished to bring to your table at Nonna's, so that year we bought his entire crop. It arrived here just three weeks after pressing, in cans and bottles bearing our own label – Nonna's Cucina Terra di Puglia Extra Virgin Olive Oil.

At first, it was so incredibly fiery but then it settled down. We sell it in the Cucina and use it in the restaurant. There is something romantic about using a product you have seen growing in the fields and produced by a man you shared lunch with.

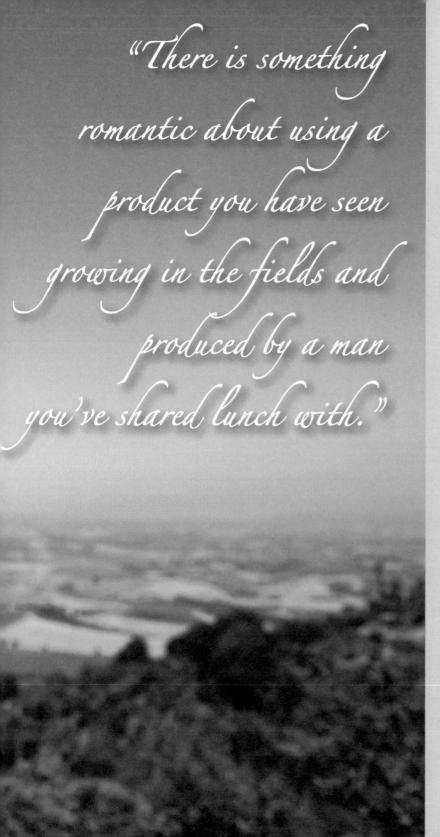

"There is something romantic about using a product you have seen growing in the fields and produced by a man you've shared lunch with."

Olive oil has been made in Italy for centuries and the story of its amazing production from ancient, gnarled trees is fascinating. The toils of the farmers, often harvesting in unbearable heat and its refinement using ancient methods is hugely symbolic of Italian culture and the nation's determination to produce quality foodstuffs almost against all odds.

A vast amount of olive oil is produced in Italy, yet amongst all the world's producers it arguably stands proudly as the best. Oils, which vary in colour and flavour from region to region according to olive variety, are made by artisan producers with a passion and dedication. Ripe olives are harvested and transported to one of the 9,000 ancient *frantoio*, or olive mills, scattered among most regions.

They are cold pressed (warmth harms the oil) and the oil extracted.

Most people know that "extra virgin oil" is the top quality but few know it refers to the product's acidity. For this classification the oil must be less than 0.5 per cent. This can only be ensured if the olives are picked by hand before they are fully ripened and the process of cold pressing completed as soon as possible.

Extra virgin olive oil is best used in dressing or drizzled directly onto food before serving and not in cooking as heat causes a chemical reaction. For cooking use simple *olio d'oliva* made from hot pressing. It's cheaper and doesn't lose its qualities when it gets hot in the pan.

Salone del GUSTO

I was once on a wine tasting trip with a former Nonna's chef, Nic Long, and we stopped in a hotel and restaurant in Bra, Piemonte. This is the town where the remarkable 'Slow Food Movement' began in 1989. It is a non-profit organisation set up specifically to combat fast food, fast life, the disappearance of local food traditions and people's dwindling interest in the food and wine they eat and drink, where it comes from, how it tastes and how our choices affect the rest of the world.

For people as passionate about these principles, as we are, it is like manna from heaven.

It's something we have embraced in our Cucina and our whole approach to the use of local products in the restaurant wherever possible.

Every two years the movement holds a magnificent show of force – the amazing Salone del Gusto, held in Turin.

This is the Good Food Show, Italian style. The fair involves cooks, wine specialists, restaurateurs, journalists and experts, with an increasing number of devoted visitors and fans.

Go there and witness rows and rows of salamis, Parma hams, hundreds of cheeses you have never seen or heard of before and wines that often do not get bottled – let alone exported.

A gourmet there is like a child in a sweet shop; it is a mind blowing experience. We can't recommend a visit to the Salone del Gusto highly enough.

Nonna's TIRAMISU

Serves six

Tiramisu has been on our menu from the start and is one of the most frequently requested recipes by our customers – though we have kept it a secret until now!

Ingredients

for the base:
18 savoiardi biscuits
150ml strong espresso
5tbsp marsala

for the mascarpone cream:
3 large free-range eggs
  (separate eggs from yolks)
5tbsp sugar
250g mascarpone
100ml whipping cream

Cocoa for dusting

Method

Place the 3 egg yolks in a large bowl with the sugar and whisk until very pale.

Add the mascarpone and the cream to the bowl and beat until thickened.

In a separate bowl, whisk 2 egg whites until peaks are formed.

Slowly add the whisked egg whites to the mascarpone cream, folding gently, mixing well but lightly.

The cream should be soft and airy.

Now mix the marsala and the espresso – dip each side of the savoiardi biscuits one by one in the marsala/espresso, still keeping the savoiardi firm.

To assemble, layer the biscuits in a glass, then add cream, followed by another biscuit until full, finish with a layer of cream.

Sprinkle cocoa powder on top to finish.

Brutti ma buoni
AL COCCO

Coconut Macaroons - makes 10-12 biscuits

The name means 'ugly but nice' as the original style looked less appetising. This is one style of biscuit we make for the coffee bar.

Ingredients

4 egg whites
200g sugar
200g coconut
Pinch of salt

Method

Whisk the egg whites while adding the sugar a bit at a time, add a pinch of salt and whisk until semi-firm peaks are formed.

Delicately add the coconut shavings.

Put the mixture in a piping bag and slowly form round shaped macaroons.

Freeze until hard.

Pre-heat the oven to 150°c.

Bake the macaroons straight from the freezer — if you were to bake them immediately after forming them, they would go flat.

Bake for 30-35 minutes.

NONNA'S INDICE

Castel del Monte, Historic Centre

Via Castel del Monte – Andria (Bari)
Tel. 0039 (0)883 569997 - (0)805 286237
www.casteldelmonte.net
info@ennepi.it
A stunning Puglian castle standing proud and solitary on a rocky summit overlooking the Murge hills shown to me by Mimmo, the son of our olive oil producer, on a tour of Puglia. The surrounding area is full of up and coming wine producers using the local grape varities like Nero Troia, one to sample if you get the chance.

Salone del Gusto

Torino
Tel. 0039 (0)172 419611
www.salonedelgusto.com
Held every two years in the Lingotto, an old Fiat factory in Turin, this is a gastronomic heaven. Halls upon halls of artisan products, ranging from biscotti to mountains of cheeses; the wine hall and sampling enoteca could take a day in itself.
The surrounding areas of Barolo and Alba, famous for white truffles, are close by and would round off a fantastic food expedition.

Cantine Ascheri Giacomo

Via G. Piumati, 23 – 12042 Bra (Cn)
Open; Tues – Fri noon – 2pm; 7.30pm – 11pm;
Sat and Sun; 7.30pm – 11pm. Closed Mon.
Tel. 0039 (0)172 412394
www.ascherivini.it
Wine makers Ascheri have a truly traditional osteria, or tavern, where the menu entirely features Piedmontese dishes. The osteria tavern has wonderful old wooden tables and you can buy wine by the glass.

Osteria del Boccon di Vino

Via Mendicita' 14
12042 Bra (CN)
Closed Sun and Mon (open Sun in Oct and Nov)
Tel. 0039 (0)172 425674
www.boccondivinoslow.it or www.slowfood.com
Bra, the small Piemonte town, is the home to the start of the 'slow food' movement, a convivium to retain the principles of artisan food production. This restaurant is where it all started, and the office sits below the restaurant.
As you would expect, great rustic food with a vast selection of older vintage Barolos from the regions top producers.

Ponte Vecchio, Florence

CHAPTER six

Casa di NONNA'S

The phone rang one evening and on the line was Michael Hackett , an old friend and a Nonna's regular over the years.

There was a hubbub in the background and it sounded as if he was in a busy bar somewhere. In fact he was in a restaurant in Milan and he couldn't understand what was on the menu because it was all in Italian and wanted help with translation!

It's a typical story of the sort of relationships we have developed with customers in Nonna's, many whom have become friends.

Often we would get customers coming in with a map and asking for tips on where in Italy they should visit. They knew our love of real Italy, away from the tourist track and they wanted a piece of it for themselves. We were becoming a bit like an unofficial tourist board.

We had considered buying a property in Italy, and all these requests for information made us think.

Why didn't we buy a house so we would have somewhere we could send everybody?

We had the ideal contact in Maurizio's father...

It started a search for a property which ended in us acquiring a home in Tuscany which we have named Casa di Nonna's.

It is the stuff of storybooks. The house is perched high in the hills in Northern Tuscany far away from the tourist track, yet within easy reach of some of the most historic places. It has lots of land, fabulous views, peace and tranquillity.

The house has an interesting, yet tragic history which tells a wider story of rural Italy.

For generations it had been a smallholding under the ownership of one family. The peace and quiet of the area was shattered in 1944 when the retreating German army's scorched earth tactic saw them raze buildings to the ground.

The house was set alight and the family's father and mother were murdered. One of the daughters survived by hiding in the woods and she eventually returned to rebuild the property. Today, a plaque stands on the wall in memory of those killed in a tragic period of Italian history.

The years after the war saw a migration of the younger element of Italy's rural communities to the cities where they sought work and a better standard of living.

Many of the hillside properties became redundant and dilapidated, and ours was no exception.

Eventually the family that had owned the house for generations looked to sell, and that is where we came in. The family kept a flat on one part of the property and we bought the rest and added the cherry house on land occupied by a derelict rabbit hutch and cattle shed.

We were the first strangers, or stranieri, ever to have ownership of the land but we all get on well and are now firm family friends.

The family still have their flat and they come up at the weekend to tend the allotment where they grow gorgeous tomatoes and salad stuff.

It is lovely having them there and they have been our introduction to the local community.

The area is very beautiful and green and gives a slightly cooler respite from the Italian hot summer heat, yet it's in easy reach of Florence, Pisa, Lucca and Modena and the nearby beautiful towns such as Montecatini, Pescia and Velano and Vinci, the birthplace of one of the most famous Italians of all, Leonardo.

I find it an almost spiritual place; somewhere to relax on trips with Melanie and our families and absorb the joys of traditional rural Italian life where people's enjoyment comes from the simple things – family life, community spirit and of course good food and wine.

Sitting in my hammock looking to the hills, listening to the tolling of the four clocktowers in the distance; it's a magical place, a land of porcini, fresh herbs, ripe figs and pears and even wild boar and crested porcupines.

IN MEMORIA
DI
GIULIO MARIANI
N UNO CON LA SORELLA ELETTA
IL 17 AGOSTO 1944
SSO LE ROVINE DI QUESTA SUA CASA
RUCIDATO DAL TEDESCO INVASORE
IL FIGLIO MARINO MARIANI
UN ANNO DOPO
VOLLE
L'EDIFICIO RISORTO

parmigiano REGGIANO

The characteristic aroma of Parmigiano-Reggiano was one of my earliest sensory images from my holidays in Italy, and in particular from the time we spent in Granny's deli. She would always stock whole wheels of the cheese of varying maturity, each weighing between 35 and 40 kilos. As kids we would cut off pieces to eat, learning to acquire the taste for its sharp, complex fruity, nutty flavour and its slightly gritty texture. Parmesan cheese, as the English and French know it incorrectly, is a true symbol of Italy. It is used everywhere, and imitated by many.

The traditional cheese, protected by a 'Denominazione d'Origine Protetta' (DOP), a guarantee by the European Union to promote the authenticity and genuine characteristics of certain food and agricultural products, is made only in the provinces of Parma, Reggio Emilia, Modena and Bologna.

We went to Azienda Agricola Montecoppe in Collecchio, Emilia-Romagna to see how it is made.

There are strict rules concerning its production. For example the cows that supply the milk must only be fed on grass and hay and from then on the cheese undergoes a production method virtually unchanged from medieval days.

After a year's maturation each cheese is inspected invididually by an expert whose approach is not unlike a doctor checking a patient's reflexes. A special hammer is used to tap the rind in various places and the inspector simply listens to the response from his blows. Cheeses are then approved or rejected. Some go on for further maturation which affects hardness, texture and flavour.

When buying, look out for the distinctive logo of the Consorzio Formaggio Parmigiano-Reggiano which identifies the cheese as genuine.

Parmesan is delicious grated over most pasta dishes, but not those with seafood. It is also excellent with fruit such as pears and figs, or dressed with a little balsamic vinegar.

Montaione
A HAVEN FOR THE SOUL

In recent years the Italian government has been keen to promote and subsidise Agriturismo in an attempt to halt migration from the countryside.

A great example of how this has benefited visitors is in Sorano, an amazing hilltop town near to Casa di Nonna's.

Sorano is a collection of little houses and a towering fortress sitting on top of a giant rock overlooking the Lente river valley.

As the road winds upwards perilously towards town, you pass fields of tall plants resembling bamboo. These are the famous milky-white fagiolo di Sorana, a delicacy that has earned them the prestigious 'Indicazione Geografica Protetta' (IGP) mark, a similar EU quality guarantee as the DOP.

Throughout history the Sorano people have been called "the bean-eaters" and the tradition lives on.

I was first taken there one Sunday to a restaurant called Agriturismo Montaione packed with families at long tables enjoying lunch.

This was Agriturismo at its finest. Local antipasti, crostini, home made pasta with wild boar, tagliatelle with mushrooms, olive oil and parsley, main courses of roast rabbit, chicken, beef and wild boar all washed down with flasks of local wine. And, of course… the beans.

The feast was followed by Grappa, huge chunks of local cheese and coffee. As much as you can eat and drink for 22 euros, and just 45 minutes away from Casa di Nonna's.

Wild Boar RAGU

Serves six

Classic Tuscan food - try it with a good young Chianti.

Ingredients

3 tbsp olive oil

2 onions (finely chopped)

1 clove garlic (crushed)

10 juniper berries

1 pinch fresh grated nutmeg

1 pinch fresh ground cinnamon

4 bay leaves

500g peeled plum tomatoes (chopped)

1kg minced wild boar

300ml red wine

150ml chicken stock

Method

In a large pan heat the olive oil.

Add the mince and seal it off.

When the mince is golden brown pour it into a sieve to drain off the excess fat.

Return the pan to the heat, add the onion, garlic, juniper, nutmeg, cinnamon, bay leaves, plum tomatoes, red wine & chicken stock.

Cook out for five minutes until the onion is tender.

Return the mince to the pan, stir together.

Season, bring up to the boil.

Turn down to simmer & cook until sauce is thick & rich.

The ragu is best served with tagliatelle & shaved pecorino.

il fagiolo
DI SORANA IGP

Italian produce has a story to tell, no more so than the Sorana bean. The small pearly white, tender and delicate bean has such a thin smooth skin that it almost melts in the mouth.

It is has been prized by all Tuscans and many famous Italians over the years. Composer Gioacchino Rossini once asked to be paid for one of his scores in Sorana beans.

They are grown in the land along the Pescia river, described as "Pescian Switzerland" because it is located in a dense green wooded area, which stretches from the Ponte di Sorana to Ponte di Castelvecchio. The plant can reach five metres in height. The microclimate and characteristics of the soil, called "ghiareto" make for the perfect environment to grow the beans, which are looked after like the most precious of vineyards.

By tradition sowing takes place during the last moon of May and on the days of the week that don't contain the letter "r".

A legend has it that if you sow on a day with the letter "r" the bean will go black. They are harvested between August and September solely by hand, after which they are sun-dried for four days. Finally, they are carefully selected and confectioned with grains of black pepper and sometimes a few laurel leaves.

It is advisable to soak the bean in water the evening before cooking and then boil them in the same water, preferably in a "gozzo" (a wide mouth glass bottle) or in a traditional terracotta pan.

How to cook

Soak 300g of the beans in clear water overnight.

Place the beans with 50g of extra virgin Tuscan olive oil, 5 sage leaves & two cloves of unpeeled garlic in the "gozzo".

Season with salt and fill three quarters full with the water.

Tap the bottle with cotton and tie with string so that it cannot come open.

Place on a low heat as the beans must cook but never boil.

When all the water is evaporated, they are ready.

Serve with a light dressing of oil and black pepper.

Pappa al POMODORO &SUGO

This Zuppa (soup) is one of my favourites and yet is so quick and easy to prepare. It epitomises the 'Cucina Povera' using up all the leftovers to great effect, providing a nutritious and healthy meal.

Ingredients

20 ripe vine tomatoes
3 dried chillies (chopped)
3 garlic cloves (chopped)
1 pint of Sugo (see below)
drizzle of good quality extra virgin olive oil
4 finely diced shallots
basil
Stale Tuscan bread

Method

Peel and de-seed tomatoes and roughly chop.

Gently sweat the shallots, garlic and chillies until soft.

Add tomatoes and warm through until tomatoes start to break.

Add the Sugo.

Season and finish with torn basil and chunks of crustless white bread and good olive oil.

Sugo Ingredients

1 carrot (diced)
1 onion (diced)
2 sticks of celery (diced)
6 cloves garlic (chopped)
1kg ripe vine tomatoes
large bunch of basil
salt & pepper
olive oil

Method

Sweat the carrot, onion and celery mix with the garlic in olive oil using a thick bottom pan until soft.

Add the vine tomatoes and cook together on a low heat stirring frequently.

Add the basil and season then push whole mixture through a sieve.

Antico Colle

10 Piazza Cavour Colle – Buggiano,
Near Montecatini, Pistoia, Tuscany
Tel. 0039 (0)572 30671
Small hilltop village with ancient towers, this restaurant set in the small Piazza with outside tables in the summer, good pizza, local soups like Pappa Pomodoro. Tagliata di manzo (steak), topped with porcini is a must!

Grotta Giusti Terme & Hotel,

Via Grotta Giusti 1411, 51015 Monsummano Terme,
Tel. 0039 (0)572 90771
Famous thermal spring heated outdoor pool and 'Inferno caves' to sweat out your toxins if you've been indulging in too much local wine.

Caffè – Ristorante Giusti

Piazza Giusti, 24
51010 – Montecatini Alto, Pistoia
Tel. 0039 (0)572 70186
www.cafferistorantegiusti.it
Set in the picturesque Montecatini Alto Piazza, the best way to get up there is by the finiculare from Montecatini Terme. The ravioli with ricotta and sage butter is a light dish to have while sitting in the sunshine, although a little bit touristy it's well worth taking the time to enjoy the surroundings.

Casa di Nonna's

Podere, Ercole
218 Via Malminnese, Ponte de Velano,
Pescia, Tuscany
www.casadinonnas.com
Our secret hideaway, that is unfortunately no longer a secret. The views and tranquility continue to amaze me and many a lunch has been spent gazing over the surrounding landscape.
A great base to visit the marvels of the area, Florence, Lucca, Pisa, Vinci to name but a few.
Book early as the word is out!

the day of the party SALUTE!

For a decade I had longed to share my 40th birthday celebrations with my family and friends, and Casa di Nonna's provided me with the perfect setting to make my dream come true.

About 40 of my family and dearest friends flew over to Italy for a party to remember.

My aunties in Italy, Gabby and Lidia, and the friends we had made at the Casa all played a part in a memorable occasion. Melanie joined in using her interior design skills to great effect, decorating tables and creating a true party atmosphere.

Maurizio, who was supposed to be working in England, made a surprise visit accompanied by our great friend, Adrian Bagnoli.

The preparations began about a week before the party when Leo, the old boy next door, and his friends took me hunting for porcini in the woods behind the house.

Armed with big baskets and walking sticks we set off at 7am in search of our elusive treasure. These men are experts at gathering porcini. We walked for about 20 minutes into the woods and soon they started finding them. I just don't know how they managed to pick them out. Camouflaged among the fallen autumn leaves I couldn't find even one. Eventually I picked up the knack and we ended up with the biggest find they have had in years. I returned to the Casa, a proud "hunter-gatherer", to show off our haul piled in baskets.

In Italy they find 101 things to do with any product and porcini is no exception. Next day we enjoyed porcini omelette for breakfast.

By this time the Casa was a hive of activity. My aunties from Modena had arrived and they spent the whole week preparing food for the party.

They made crespelle ai funghi trifolati e asparagi – pancakes with some of the porcini, layered with asparagus and béchamel in big trays. Then together we started to make huge lasagne sheets with their rolling pins using 10 eggs per kilo to the dough and adding chopped, boiled spinach.

Then they made the ragu like Nonna used to make and finally the béchamel sauce. It was a long process but a fantastic way to spend the day.

For wine we took some huge demijohns to a local producer in Montecarlo, just five minutes away. He's a friend of a friend who doesn't bother to bottle his wine and it cost only one euro a litre!

When my birthday arrived we all sat down at a big long table, enjoyed our simple but fabulous feast and spent five hours relaxing and simply having fun. It was a magical day that will remain in my memory forever.

We started with Parma ham and ripe figs from a tree in the garden, followed by the crepelle and lasagne.

Then came three inch thick Bistecca alla Fiorentina bought from a good butcher nearby.

Dressed with a little olive oil and rock salt they were cooked by Leo on an open grill, fired by olive twigs and served simply with grilled courgettes and aubergines.

For dessert we had pecorino with pears from the garden and local honey.

It was a personal celebration for me but also a celebration of Italian culture. Simple food and drink that didn't cost the earth in the company of your family and close friends.

"...We all sat down at a big long table & enjoyed our simple but fabulous feast"

the *perfect* STEAK

World famous Florentine steak – a huge T-Bone with a sirloin on one side of the bone and the fillet on the other – has an ancient breed of cattle once featured in Roman sculptures to thank for it popularity.

In its truest form a Florentine steak comes only from Chianina cattle – massive, sturdy and distinctive looking white beasts reared originally in the Chiana Valley in Southern Tuscany.

Wherever I go in the world I try a steak and I can say without a shadow of a doubt that genuine Bistecca alla Fiorentina is up there with the best.

I've had Aberdeen Angus and all the famous UK and European breeds, prime grade A New York strips and Wagyu.

Yet the Chianina is without doubt in the top echelon.

I will never forget the first time I came face to face with one of the huge beasts.

We had visited La Pineta near Marina di Bibbona and over the meal we asked Luciano if he knew where we could find Chianina cattle, as we knew they were reared in the area. With a beam on his face he told us his friend was the best breeder in the region and he insisted on taking us to meet him. He drove us a short distance to the farm where we met his friend and his prize winning cattle.

The biggest animal, his pure white highly prized trophy winner, stood six feet tall and two and a half feet across. It weighed 850 kilos – that's nine of me!

La BAITA

At the back of Casa di Nonna's there is a restaurant which we make a beeline for every time we are there.

La Baita is a bit of a devil to find, tucked away in the hills above Montecatini but it is well worth the effort to visit. To make life easier for visitors to the Casa, its location is programmed into the sat-nav.

I was first taken there by Maurizio's father, whose brother Marciso had discovered it when he was training the restaurant owner Sandro Piattelli to be a parachutist.

Sandro has since become a great friend and has opened many doors for us.

There is no menu or wine list at La Baita, but here you will find one of the best steaks you will ever eat.

They will bring out the Bistecca alla Fiorentina for you to choose your steak, which is sold by the kilo. They are all about two inches thick, seasoned simply with a little rock salt, pepper and olive oil before being put into a simple wood burning oven.

It's seared with a lovely scorched crust on the outside, yet it is blood rare in the middle.

Here they also have a delicious antipasta of bresaola served with golden capped Olivetti mushrooms drizzled with olive oil and served on wooden plates.

I always ask the waiter for a wine he would recommend and it was here we first discovered the wonderful Capatosta from Poggio Argentiera and now we are the main UK outlet for the producer in the north of England. By strange coincidence, our Capatosta importer recently asked us if we would like to try one of his new wines – the very same Caparsini Chianti Classico which was the first wine we ever had on Nonna's wine list 12 years previously!

bistecca alla FIORENTINA

Bistecca alla Fiorentina from Chianina cattle is a T-bone steak with part sirloin and part fillet. It is usually 1.2-1.5kg in weight and 6 to 10cm thick.

The secret to getting the best tasting steak is the way it's cooked.

The Fiorentina is a perfect match for hot coals from hardwood with a thin layer of ash and no flames.

It is better not to season the meat beforehand so not to toughen the flesh, once cooked, every bite must give you the feeling it melts in your mouth.

- *Cook each side for 3-5 minutes, turning it only once on each side so to cook it rare.*
- *After, sit the cut on its bone and cook until the blood has drained from the bone.*
- *Rest the Fiorentina for a few minutes, add salt and pepper and brush lightly with some rosemary, if you want to add an extra flavour.*
- *Serve by trimming the fillet and contro-filet from the bone (note how rare the meat is) and then slice the pieces crosswise into 1cm slices.*
- *Accompany with cannellini & sorana beans.*

Trattoria La Baita

Localita Canfittori, via Marlianese, 72
51010 Massa E Cozzile (PT)
Tel. 0039 (0)572 66275

Consistently one of my favourite restaurants for a true Florentine steak. Difficult to find above the hills of Montecatini but well worth the effort.

Fattoria del Buonamico

Via Provinciale di Montecarlo, 43 55015 Montecarlo (Lucca)
Tel. 0039 (0)583 22038
www.buonamico.it

A small producer in the heart of Montecarlo, I was recommended these wines while dining at Cecco Restaurant in Pescia. So impressed, that the next day I knocked on the door of Fattoria del Buonamico and the genial Vasco gave me a tasting of the whole range. Particularly impressive are the Vasario and the Cercatio.

Twiga Club

Via Roma 2,
Marina di Pietrasanta,
55044, (Lucca)
Versilia
Tel. 0039 (0)584 21518
www.twigaclub.it

Owned by Formula 1 boss Flavio Briatore and Italian national football coach Marcello Lippi. Twiga is the epitomy of style. In the summer this chic beach club has Balinese beds to lounge in outside. In the winter guests enjoy its intimate interior where waiters bring premier spirits and champagne to your table.

Villa La Nina

Via S.Martino, 54
55015, Montecarlo, Tuscany
Tel. 0039 (0)583 22018
www.lanina.it

A small restaurant with ten rooms, with all the small wine producers of the area close-by. The kitchen is open and you can see the wood burning stove with local dishes being prepared. The rooms are great value for money and it's a good base to visit the surrounding area.

Crespelle ai funghi TRIFOLATI e ASPARAGI

Lasagne of pancakes with truffled wild mushrooms & asparagus – Serves six people

Ingredients

for the pancakes:

250ml milk

120g flour

50g butter

2 eggs

salt

for the layers

600g of wild mushrooms

extra virgin olive oil

flat leaf parsley

2 garlic cloves

24 month aged parmigiano-reggiano

1 bunch of asparagus (steamed)

for the besciamella

500ml milk

100g flour

50g butter

salt & pepper

nutmeg

Method

Making the pancakes:

In a small pan melt the butter and leave to cool. In the meantime put your eggs in a mixing bowl, salt the flour and slowly add the milk, just a little at a time, whilst whisking. Once cold, add the butter and finish mixing.

Melt a spoonful of butter in a pan, if there is too much melted butter keep some on the side to lubricate the pan after a few pancakes. When the pan is hot, pour in a ladle of the pancake mixture. As soon as the batter hits the hot pan, tip it around from side to side to get the base evenly coated with batter.

It takes only a few minutes for the batter to cook, lift it with a palette knife and turn it onto the other side. Leave to cook for half a minute until golden brown. Simply turn it out onto a plate.

Continue making pancakes until the batter is finished.

Making the besciamella:

Besciamella is a white creamy sauce used to make lasagne, it's so versatile, it can be utilised for any al forno dish. Pour the milk in a pot, with a very low fire and add your butter, to melt. When the butter is almost all melted, start adding your flour bit by bit whilst whisking. Whisk until the flour is incorporated, then add seasoning and a teaspoon of grounded nutmeg. Mix for a further 5 minutes, until smooth. Remove from heat, sprinkle a handful of parmigiano reggiano, stir slightly and set aside for later.

For the funghi trifolati & asparagus:

Chop a generous amount of parsley along with two cloves of garlic.

In a pan, pour a splash of olive oil, add your mushrooms and garlic, turn your hob to a gentle heat, cook for 3-4 minutes, stirring from time to time. Add seasoning and a knob of butter.

Finally add chopped parsley to the pan and cook for a further 30 seconds, so to allow the parsley to flavour the mushrooms. It's the chopped garlic and parsley that make the mushroom truffled or trifolati.

Remove from heat and let it rest.

Add your asparagus to boiling salted water for around 2 minutes – you want them to be lightly crunchy as they will do their final cooking time together with the crespelle.

Once ready, put in a bowl of cold water and put on one side.

Assembling the dish:

You will need a rectangular oven dish with a depth of 8-10cm and approximately 30cm long.

Get your pancakes and cut in half so to get sheet like layers – Put a couple of ladles of besciamella in the oven dish and spread it evenly.

Lay your pancake sheets to form the first layer then add a generous portion of mushrooms and asparagus. Pour some besciamella on top & sprinkle generously with parmesan – repeat until there are no more pancakes left.

Pour on top any besciamella, mushroom and asparagus left and finish off with more parmesan.

This layer of parmesan, once grilled, will create a delicious crust.

Bake in an oven at 200ºc for around 30 minutes.

Lasagne della NONNA

Serves eight people

Ingredients

for the Ragu

700g mince (mixed between pork and veal)

1 carrot

1 onion

1 stick of celery

olive oil

salt pepper

400g tomato passata (conserva)

for the Besciamella

½ ltr of milk

50g plain flour

knob of butter

salt & pepper

ground nutmeg

handful of parmigiano-reggiano

for the pasta

300g plain flour

2 large eggs

handful freshly boiled spinach (drained of water, chopped)

Method

To make the ragu:

Place the carrot, onion and celery in a pan and fry in olive oil for two minutes - add the mince. Season and fry the soffritto mix until browned.

Add the tomato passata and cook on a low heat for 3 hours.

To make the Besciamella:

Slowly melt the butter in a deep pan and then slowly add the flour - mix well.

Slowly add the milk bringing it very gently to the boil, stirring all the while until it thickens.

Add a pinch of ground nutmeg, salt and pepper, knob of butter and handful of parmigiano-reggiano.

Stir in and set aside.

To make the pasta:

Add the eggs and spinach to the flour - mix until a dough is formed.

Roll the dough out on floured surface until thin (not too thin).

Cut into 10 large rectangles.

Bringing the recipe together:

Cook the pasta into plenty boiling salted water, two or three rectangles at the time and boil for 3 minutes.

Drain the rectangles of pasta and allow to dry. Repeat until all rectangles are done.

Grease a large rectangular oven proof dish with butter - place two rectangles to cover the bottom of the oven dish.

Add a layer of besciamella, then a layer of ragu, finish layer with parmigiano. Repeat until you have five completed layers.

Cook in the middle of the oven at 180ºc for 40 minutes or a bit longer if you want crustier top. When ready leave to stand for 5 minutes.